UNLOCK THE SECRETS TO FINANCIAL FREEDOM AND TRANSFORM YOUR FUTURE

Adefemi Ogundana

2 unlock the secrets to financial freedom and transform your future

COPYRIGHT

Copyright © 2024 Adefemi Ogundana

All rights reserved. No part of this book may be reproduced, distributed, or transmitted in any form or by any means, including photocopying, recording, or other electronic or mechanical methods, without the prior written permission of the publisher, except in the case of brief quotations embodied in critical reviews and certain other non-commercial uses permitted by copyright law.

DEDICATION

This book is dedicated to God Almighty.

To the Memory of My Father and Mother

ACKNOWLEDGMENT

My sincere gratitude to my darling husband, Kayode your unwavering love and support throughout the journey of writing this book. Your belief in me has been a beacon of light during the darkest hours and a constant source of strength when I needed it most. I am forever grateful to you, my love and best friend.

I wish to say thank you to my family, for their patience, understanding and Love. Your encouragement and confidence in my abilities kept me going even when I doubted myself.

PREFACE

Welcome to "Unlock the Secrets to Financial Freedom and Transform Your Future." This book is designed to guide you on a comprehensive journey towards achieving financial independence and long-term wealth. Whether you are just starting to manage your finances or looking to refine your existing strategies, this book provides practical insights, proven strategies, and actionable steps to help you reach your financial goals.

The path to financial freedom is a combination of knowledge, discipline, and mindset. Over the years, I've seen countless individuals struggle with their finances, not because they lack the potential to succeed, but because they lack the right information and guidance. My motivation for writing this book stems from a deep desire to demystify the complexities of personal finance and provide a clear, actionable roadmap that anyone can follow.

In this book, you will find:

Fundamental Concepts: We start with the basics, ensuring you have a solid understanding of essential financial principles such as budgeting, saving, and investing. These chapters lay the groundwork for more advanced strategies.

Advanced Strategies: As you progress, you'll learn about sophisticated investment techniques, how to create multiple streams of income, and methods for managing debt wisely. These strategies are designed to maximize your wealth-building potential.

Mindset and Habits: Financial success is not just about numbers; it's also about developing the right mindset and habits. You'll discover how to overcome financial fears, adopt a millionaire mindset, and cultivate the habits of successful individuals.

Long-Term Planning: We delve into crafting a comprehensive financial plan that includes retirement planning, estate planning, and protecting your wealth. These chapters ensure that your financial success is sustainable and secure.

Each chapter is structured to provide clear, step-by-step guidance, practical tips, and real-life examples. I've also included tools and resources to help you implement the strategies discussed, making it easier for you to take control of your financial future.

The journey to financial freedom is unique for everyone, and there is no one-size-fits-all approach. However, the principles and strategies outlined in this book are adaptable and can be customized to fit your individual circumstances. My hope is that, by the end of this book, you will feel empowered, informed, and ready to take the steps necessary to transform your financial future.

Thank you for choosing this book as your guide. I am excited to embark on this journey with you and look forward to seeing the transformation it brings to your life. Remember, financial freedom is within your reach—let's unlock the secrets together.

Adefemi Ogundana

TABLE OF CONTENTS

COPYRIGHT 3
DEDICATION 4
ACKNOWLEDGMENT 5
PREFACE 6
INTRODUCTION 11
   The path to financial freedom 11
CHAPTER 1 14
   Setting Your Financial Goals 14
   Conclusion 19
CHAPTER 2 20
   Mastering Personal Budgeting 20
   Conclusion 26
CHAPTER 3 28
   Saving Strategies for Wealth Accumulation 28
   Conclusion 35
CHAPTER 4 36
   Investing Fundamentals 36
   Conclusion 43
CHAPTER 5 44
   Advanced Investment Techniques 44
   Conclusion 50
CHAPTER 6 51
   Generating Passive Income Streams 51

9 unlock the secrets to financial freedom and transform your future

Conclusion 58
CHAPTER 7 59
Managing Debt Wisely 59
Conclusion 66
CHAPTER 8 67
Developing a Millionaire Mindset 67
Conclusion 71
CHAPTER 9 73
Crafting Your Long-Term Financial Plan 73
Conclusion 77
CHAPTER 10 78
Creating Multiple Streams of Income 78
Conclusion 83
CHAPTER 11 84
Maintaining Financial Freedom 84
Conclusion 89

INTRODUCTION

The path to financial freedom

Welcome to "Unlock the Secrets to Financial Freedom and Transform Your Future." This book is your guide to achieving the financial independence you've always dreamed of. Whether you're just starting your financial journey or looking to refine your existing strategies, this book offers the insights, tools, and strategies you need to take control of your finances and build lasting wealth.

understanding financial freedom

Financial freedom means different things to different people. For some, it's about having enough money to live comfortably without worrying about bills. For others, it's the ability to pursue passions and dreams without being tied to a job solely for financial reasons. At its core, financial freedom is about having control over your finances rather than being controlled by them.

Achieving financial freedom involves more than just accumulating wealth. It requires a shift in mindset, adopting the right habits, and making informed decisions that align with your long-term goals. This book will help you understand these principles and put them into practice.

The Importance of a Wealth Mindset

A wealth mindset is crucial for financial success. It's about seeing opportunities instead of obstacles, focusing on long-term gains instead of short-term pleasures, and believing in your ability to create and sustain wealth. Developing a wealth mindset involves changing the way you think about money, success, and yourself.

Throughout this book, we will explore how to cultivate a millionaire mindset, overcome financial fears and limiting beliefs, and adopt the habits of successful individuals. By changing your mindset, you'll be better equipped to make smart financial decisions and stay motivated on your path to financial freedom.

How This Book Will Guide You

This book is structured to provide you with a comprehensive roadmap to financial freedom. Each chapter builds on the previous one, guiding you through essential concepts, practical strategies, and actionable steps to achieve your financial goals.

Embark on this journey with an open mind and a commitment to making positive changes in your financial life. Financial freedom is within your reach—let's unlock the secrets together.

CHAPTER 1

Setting Your Financial Goals

The ability to think about or plan the future with foresight and creative mind will lead to a world of financial freedom. Setting well-defined financial goals is the foundation upon which all other financial decisions are made. In this chapter, we'll explore the process of setting both short-term and long-term financial goals, the importance of SMART goals, and how to create a personal finance roadmap that guides you towards financial success.

Defining Short-term and Long-term Goals

Short-term Goals: Short-term goals are financial targets you aim to achieve within the next year. These might include saving for a vacation, building an emergency fund, paying off a credit card, or purchasing new household items. These goals are often the stepping stones that lead to larger, long-term objectives.

Long-term Goals: Long-term goals are financial aspirations that span over several years, often ranging from five years to several decades. Common long-term goals include saving for retirement, buying a home, funding a child's education, or achieving financial independence. These goals require consistent effort, planning, and time to accomplish.

The Balance Between Short-term and Long-term Goals

While it's important to focus on long-term financial health, short-term goals keep you motivated and provide immediate satisfaction. Balancing both types of goals ensures that you're making progress now while planning.

SMART Goals for Financial Success

Setting goals is more effective when they are SMART: Specific, Measurable, Achievable, Relevant, and Time-bound. This approach adds clarity and accountability to your financial objectives.

Specific: A specific goal clearly states what you want to achieve. Instead of saying, "I want to save money," a specific goal would be, "I want to save $5,000 for a down payment on a car."

Measurable: Measurable goals allow you to track your progress. For example, "I will save $400 each month to reach my $5,000 goal in 12 months." This provides a clear metric to monitor.

Achievable: Achievable goals are realistic and attainable. Consider your current financial situation and resources. Setting a goal to save $1 million in a year might not be feasible but saving $10,000 could be.

Relevant: Relevant goals align with your values and long-term objectives. Ask yourself why the goal is important and how it fits into your broader financial plan.

Time-bound: Time-bound goals have a deadline. This urgency encourages consistent progress. For example, "I will save $5,000 by December 31, 2024."

Creating a Personal Finance Roadmap

A personal finance roadmap is a strategic plan that outlines the steps needed to achieve your financial goals. Here's how to create one:

1. Assess Your Current Financial Situation:

List all sources of income.

Detail your monthly expenses.

Calculate your net worth by subtracting liabilities from assets.

2. Set Your Financial Goals:

Write down both short-term and long-term goals using the SMART criteria.

Set your goals priority base on their importance and urgency.

3. Develop a Budget:

Create a budget that aligns with your goals. Ensure that you allocate funds towards savings and debt repayment.

The use of budgeting tools will assist you in coordinating your finances effective and efficiently.

4. Implement Savings Strategies

Automate your savings to ensure consistency.

Explore high-yield savings accounts for better returns on your savings.

5. Plan for Investments:

Educate yourself about different investment options.

Start small and gradually diversify your portfolio.

6. Monitor and Adjust Your Plan:

Always review your financial plan and modify as required.

Stay adaptable to changes in your financial situation or goals.

Staying Committed to Your Goals

Commitment is key to achieving your financial goals. Here are some tips to stay on track:

Visualize Your Goals

Create a vision board or use a financial planning app to keep your goals visible.

Celebrate Milestones

Reward yourself for reaching short-term goals. This keeps you motivated.

Seek Accountability

Share your goals with a trusted friend or join a financial group for support.

Educate Yourself:

Continuously learn about personal finance through books, courses, and seminars.

Conclusion

Setting clear financial goals is the first step on your journey to financial freedom. By defining your short-term and long-term objectives, utilizing the SMART criteria, and creating a personal finance roadmap, you lay the groundwork for achieving your dreams. Stay committed, regularly review your progress, and adjust your plans as needed. With determination and discipline, financial freedom is within your reach.

CHAPTER 2

Mastering Personal Budgeting

Budgeting is the cornerstone of financial management. It's the tool that helps you control your money, ensuring that your income is allocated effectively to meet your needs and achieve your financial goals. In this chapter, we'll delve into the basics of budgeting, the importance of tracking income and expenses, and the tools and apps that can help you manage your budget effectively.

The Basics of Budgeting

Budgeting is the written plan for how you spend and save your income every month. This spending plan is called a budget. This written plan let you to decide ahead if you will have sufficient money for other things you might need.

Here's how to get started:

1. Calculate Your Income

List all sources of income, including salary, bonuses, freelance work, rental income, and any other sources.

Calculate your total monthly income.

2. List Your Expenses:

Fixed Expenses: These are regular, unchanging costs like rent/mortgage, car payments, insurance premiums, and loan payments.

Variable Expenses: These fluctuate each month and include groceries, utilities, entertainment, and dining out.

Discretionary Expenses: Non-essential expenses such as hobbies, vacations, and luxury items.

3. Categorize Your Expenses

Organize your expenses into categories. Common categories include housing, transportation, food, utilities, savings, and entertainment.

4. Allocate Your Income:

Assign portions of your income to each expense category. Make sure that you do not spend more than your total income.

5. Set Spending Limits:

Establish limits for each expense category based on your income and financial goals. Adhere to these limits and avoid wastage.

Tracking Income and Expenses

Tracking your income and expenses is crucial for maintaining control over your finances. Here's how to do it effectively:

1. Keep Detailed Records:

Record every expense, no matter how small. Using the till receipts, bank account statements, and credit card statements for calculation and ensure accuracy.

2. Use Financial Tools:

Leverage budgeting tools and apps to track your spending automatically. Personal finance tools include Mint, YNAB (You Need a Budget), Honey dew and Personal Capital.

3. Review Regularly:

Plan for regular review monthly basis to compare actual expenses with your budget.

Look for areas where you may be overspending and adjust your budget accordingly.

4. Adjust for Variability

Some months may have higher expenses due to holidays, birthdays, or emergencies. Plan for these fluctuations by setting aside extra funds in months with lower expenses.

Tools and Apps for Effective Budget Management

In the digital age, managing your budget has never been easier thanks to a variety of tools and apps designed to help you track your finances. The popular options are as follows:

1. Mint:

Features: Mint connects to your bank accounts, credit cards, and bills to automatically track your expenses and categorize them. It helps to track your spending routine and your set financial objectives.

Benefits: Easy to use, comprehensive tracking, and free to use.

2. YNAB (You Need a Budget

Features: YNAB encourages proactive budgeting by assigning every Pound a job.

It focuses on helping users break the pay cheque-to-paycheque cycle, get out of debt, and save more money.

Benefits: Proven budgeting method, educational resources, and strong community support.

3. Personal Capital

Features: Personal Capital combines budgeting with investment tracking. It offers tools to track your spending, plan for retirement, and monitor your investment portfolio.

Benefits: Comprehensive financial overview, investment analysis, and retirement planning.

4. Pocket Guard

Features: Pocket Guard connects to your financial accounts and helps you track spending, create budgets, and identify areas where you can save money.

Benefits: User-friendly interface, spending insights, and savings tips.

5. Good budget:

Features: Good budget uses the envelope budgeting method, where you allocate funds to different categories or envelopes. It's great for those who prefer a hands-on approach to budgeting.

Benefits: Simple and intuitive, envelope system, and helps you stick to spending limits.

Tips for Sticking to Your Budget

Creating a budget is one thing, but sticking to it requires discipline and dedication. The following points will keep you on course:

1. Be Realistic:

Set realistic spending limits that reflect your lifestyle and financial goals. Unrealistic budgets can lead to frustration and failure.

2. Avoid Impulse Purchases:

Always ask yourself if you need or want what you are about to purchase. Delay non-essential purchases to give yourself time to consider their necessity.

3. Use Cash for Discretionary Spending

Have a set amount of cash withdraw for weekly spending. When the cash is gone, avoid spending until the next week.

4. Review and Adjust Regularly

Life circumstances change, and so should your budget. Reg Review and modify your budget regularly to accommodate changes in income, expenses, and goals.

5. Celebrate Milestones

Treat yourself for the success of your budget and achieving your financial goals. This will strengthen and encourage you.

Conclusion

Mastering personal budgeting is essential for achieving financial freedom. By understanding the basics of budgeting, tracking your income and expenses, and utilizing modern tools and apps, you can take control of your finances and make informed decisions. Remember, budgeting is not about restricting yourself but about making deliberate choices that align with your financial goals. Stay disciplined, be flexible, and watch as your financial health improves, and your goals come within reach.

CHAPTER 3

Saving Strategies for Wealth Accumulation

Saving money is a fundamental aspect of financial management and a key strategy for building wealth. Effective saving strategies not only provide a safety net for emergencies but also pave the way for future investments and financial freedom. In this chapter, we'll explore the power of saving early, the benefits of high-yield savings accounts and emergency funds, and the importance of automating your savings.

The Power of Saving Early

One of the most powerful tools in wealth accumulation is time. The earlier you start saving, the more time your money must grow. This concept is often referred to as the "time value of money," which highlights the potential for investments to grow exponentially over time due to compound interest.

Compound Interest: Compound interest is the interest earned on Investment saving or loan and on the earned interest. Essentially, you earn interest on your interest, leading to exponential growth over time. For example, if you save $1,500 at an annual interest rate of 5%, you'll have $1,575 at the end of the first year. In the following year, your interest will calculate on $1,575 and this continues like that.

Example: Let's consider two individuals, Alex, and Jamie. Alex starts saving $200 a month at age 25, while Jamie starts saving the same amount at age 35. Assuming an annual interest rate of 7%, by the time they both reach 65, Alex will have saved significantly more than Jamie due to the additional 10 years of compound interest working in Alex's favour.

Key Takeaways

Saving early and often will attract the full benefits of compound interest.

Every small amount of that you saved will grow substantially over time.

The longer your money is invested, the more it can grow.

Saving is not just about putting money aside; it's also about choosing the right place to store your savings. High yield

High-Yield Savings Accounts and Emergency Funds

savings accounts and emergency funds are essential. Components of a solid financial strategy

High-Yield Savings Accounts: High-yield savings accounts offer higher interest rates compared to traditional savings accounts, allowing your money to grow faster. These accounts are typically offered by online banks that have lower overhead costs and can pass the savings onto customers.

Benefits

Higher interest rates lead to greater returns on your savings.

FDIC insured, providing safety for your money.

Easy access to funds when needed.

Choosing a High-Yield Savings Account:

When selecting a high-yield savings account, consider factors such as interest rates, fees, minimum balance requirements, and accessibility. Weigh up the options and decide the to the best suit your needs.

Emergency Funds: An emergency fund is a savings buffer that protects you from unexpected financial setbacks, such as medical emergencies, car repairs, or job loss. Having an emergency fund can prevent you from going into debt when unplanned expenses arise.

Building an Emergency Fund:

Plan and save sufficient money to fund up to six months allowance.

Store your emergency fund in a high-yield savings account to ensure both easy access and higher returns.

Begin with small savings and gradually increase the amount until you achieve your target.

Benefits:

Provides financial security and peace of mind.

Maintain Financial Stability: Using your emergency fund means you don't have to worry about monthly payments and accruing interest, allowing you to maintain your financial stability.

Automating Your Savings

Automating your savings is a powerful strategy to ensure consistency and discipline in your saving habits. Set up automatic transfers from your checking account to your savings account to make saving effortless and eliminate the temptation to spend the money instead

Benefits of Automation:

Consistency: Regular, automated transfers help you save consistently without having to remember to do it manually.

Automating your savings is a powerful tool for fostering financial discipline. By removing the temptation to spend money before you save it, you ensure consistent saving habits, accelerate the achievement of your financial goals, and reduce the stress associated with financial management. Embrace automation to build a more secure and disciplined financial future.

Goal Achievement: Regular contributions help you reach your savings goals faster.

How to Automate Your Savings:

Set Up Automatic Transfers: Most banks and financial institutions allow you to set up recurring transfers from your current account to your savings account. Choose a frequency (e.g., weekly, bi-weekly, or monthly) that aligns with your income schedule.

Use Payroll Deductions: If your employer offers direct deposit, consider splitting your pay cheques so that a portion goes directly into your savings account.

Take Advantage of Apps and Tools: Many financial apps and tools can help you automate your savings. For example, apps like Capital and Acorns automatically round up your purchases to the nearest Pound and transfer the difference to your savings or investment account.

Additional Saving Strategies

In addition to the core strategies discussed above, there are several other techniques you can use to enhance your savings efforts:

1. Pay Yourself First:

Mange your savings as a basic expense, like rent or utilities. Allocate a portion of your income to savings before you spend on anything else.

Examine your expenses on monthly basis and recognise the areas you need to reduce. Redirect those savings into your savings account.

2. Cut Unnecessary Expenses

3. Increase Your Income:

Look for opportunities to boost your income, such as taking on a side hustle, freelance work, or asking for a raise. Budget more t income to your savings.

4. Take Advantage of Employer Benefits:

If your employer offers a retirement savings plan with matching contributions, such as a 401(k), contribute enough to take full advantage of the match. This is important extra money that can increase your savings.

5. Review and Adjust Your Savings Plan:

Regularly examine your savings goal and alter as need be4. Life circumstances change, and your savings plan should be flexible enough to adapt.

Conclusion

Saving money is a crucial step towards achieving financial freedom and building wealth. By understanding the power of saving early, leveraging high-yield savings accounts and emergency funds, and automating your savings, you can create a solid foundation for your financial future. Remember, saving is not just about putting money aside; it's about making deliberate choices that align with your long-term goals. Stay disciplined, review your progress regularly, and continue to seek out opportunities to enhance your savings strategies. With these practices in place, you'll be well on your way to financial success and security.

CHAPTER 4

Investing Fundamentals

Investing is an important instrument for creating wealth and establishing financial freedom. By putting your money to work through various investment vehicles, you can grow your assets over time and reach your financial goals faster. In this chapter, we will cover the basics of investing, understanding different investment vehicles, finding your risk-return balance, and building a diversified investment portfolio.

Understanding Different Investment Vehicles

Investment vehicles are the assets or instruments in which you can invest your money. Various type has its own attribute, probability, and future income. Here's an overview of the most common investment vehicles:

1. Stocks

Definition: Shares of ownership in a company. Buying a Company's stock, makes you a part-owner.

Potential Returns: High potential returns through capital appreciation and dividends.

Risks: High volatility and risk of losing principal.

2. Bonds:

Definition: Loans you give to a corporation or government in exchange for periodic interest payments and the return of the bond's face value when it matures.

Potential Returns: Lower than stocks but more stable. Returns come from fixed interest payments.

Risks: Reinvestment risk, Liquidity risk, and default risk.

3. Mutual Funds:

Definition: Pooled funds from many investors to invest in a diversified portfolio of stocks, bonds, or other securities, managed by professional fund managers.

Potential Returns: Varies depending on the fund's investments. Generally, less risky than individual stocks.

Risks: Market risk, management risk, and fees that can reduce returns.

4. Exchange-Traded Funds (ETFs):

Definition: Like mutual funds are traded on stock exchanges as individual stocks.

Potential Returns: Varies depending on the underlying assets. Typically, lower fees than mutual funds.

Risks: Market risk, liquidity risk.

5. Real Estate:

Definition: Investing in physical properties or real estate investment trusts (REITs).

Potential Returns: Rental income and property value appreciation.

Risks: Property value fluctuations, maintenance costs, and illiquidity.

6. Certificates of Deposit (CDs)

Definition: Time deposits offered by banks with a fixed interest rate and maturity date.

Potential Returns: Lower but guaranteed returns.

Risks: Low risk, but also low returns and early withdrawal penalties.

7. Cryptocurrencies:

Definition: Digital or virtual currencies that use cryptography for security and operate independently of a central bank.

Potential Returns: High potential returns due to volatility.

Risks: Extremely high risk and volatility, regulatory risk.

Risk and Return: Finding Your Balance

The knowledge of the connection between risk and return is key for making effective decision about investments. Higher potential income is associated with higher risks. Your risk tolerance will depend on your financial goals, time horizon, and personal comfort level.

1. Assess Your Risk Tolerance

Risk Tolerance Questionnaire: Many financial institutions offer questionnaires to help you assess your risk tolerance. They consider factors like age, income, investment experience, and financial goals.

Emotional Comfort: Reflect on how you've reacted to past financial losses or market downturns. Can you tolerate seeing your investments drop in value temporarily?

2. Consider Your Time Horizon:

Short-Term Goals: If you need your money within the next few years, consider low-risk investments like bonds, CDs, or high-yield savings accounts.

Long-Term Goals: For goals that are decades away, you can afford to take on more risk with investments like stocks, mutual funds, or real estate, as you have time to ride out market fluctuations.

3. Diversification:

Spreading Risk: Diversifying your investments across different asset classes, sectors, and geographies can help manage risk. If one investment performs poorly, others may perform well, balancing out your overall portfolio performance.

Building a Diversified Investment Portfolio

A diversified portfolio balances risk and return by spreading investments across various asset classes and securities. Here's how to build one:

1. Asset Allocation:

Definition: The process of dividing your investments among different asset categories, such as stocks, bonds, and cash.

Factors: Consider your risk tolerance, time horizon, and financial goals to determine the right mix of assets.

2. Rebalancing Your Portfolio:

Definition: Adjusting your portfolio periodically to maintain your desired asset allocation.

Frequency: Review your portfolio at least once a year or after significant market movements. Sell some assets and buy others to return to your target allocation.

3. Choosing Investments:

Research: Conduct thorough research before investing. Look at past performance, fees, and management quality for mutual funds and ETFs. For individual stocks, consider the company's financial health, growth prospects, and industry position.

Professional Advice: Consider consulting a financial advisor for personalized advice, especially if you're new to investing or have complex financial needs.

4. Keeping Costs Low:

Fees: High fees charges may weaken your investment income over time. Look for low-cost mutual funds and ETFs.

Taxes: Be mindful of the tax implications of your investments. Tax-efficient investing strategies, such as holding investments for more than a year to benefit from lower long-term capital gains tax rates, can help maximize your returns.

5. Staying Informed:

Education: Continuously educate yourself about investing. Read books, attend seminars, and follow financial news to stay informed about market trends and new investment opportunities.

Conclusion

Investing is a major direction in creating wealth and establishing financial freedom. By understanding different investment vehicles, assessing your risk tolerance, and building a diversified portfolio, you can make informed decisions that align with your financial goals. Remember, investing is a long-term commitment, and staying disciplined, patient, and informed is key to your success. Start small, be consistent, and watch your investments grow over time, paving the way to a secure financial future.

43 unlock the secrets to financial freedom and transform your future

CHAPTER 5

Advanced Investment Techniques

As you become more comfortable with the basics of investing, exploring advanced investment techniques can help you maximize returns and diversify your portfolio further. This chapter will delve into specific investment strategies, including stocks, bonds, mutual funds, real estate, and cryptocurrencies, to help you make informed decisions.

Stocks, Bonds, and Mutual Funds

Stocks: Advanced strategies in stock investing can significantly enhance your returns. Here are a few approaches:

Dividend Investing:

Definition: Focusing on stocks that pay regular dividends, providing a steady income stream.

Strategy: Look for companies with a history of stable and growing dividends. Reinvest dividends to buy more shares and compound your returns.

Growth Investing:

Definition: Targeting companies expected to grow at an above-average rate compared to other companies.

Strategy: Identify sectors with high growth potential (e.g., technology, biotech) and invest in companies with strong growth metrics, such as high revenue growth rates and expanding profit margins.

Value Investing:

Definition: Investing in stocks that appear undervalued based on fundamental analysis.

Strategy: Look for companies with strong fundamentals (e.g., low price-to-earnings ratios, high book values) that are temporarily out of favour with the market.

Bonds: Incorporating advanced bond strategies can help optimize your fixed-income investments.

Laddering

Definition: Creating a portfolio of bonds with different maturities.

Strategy: Invest in bonds that mature at regular intervals (e.g., every year). This approach provides liquidity and reduces interest rate risk.

Barbell Strategy:

Definition: Combining short-term and long-term bonds while avoiding intermediate maturities.

Strategy: Invest in a mix of short-term bonds for liquidity and long-term bonds for higher yields, balancing risk and return.

Duration Management:

Definition: Adjusting the duration of your bond portfolio to manage interest rate risk.

Strategy: Increase the average duration of your bonds when interest rates are expected to fall and decrease it when rates are expected to rise.

Mutual Funds and ETFs: Advanced techniques for investing in mutual funds and ETFs can enhance diversification and returns.

Sector Rotation:

Definition: Moving investments between sectors based on economic cycles.

Strategy: Invest in sectors expected to outperform during specific phases of the economic cycle (e.g., technology during growth, utilities during recessions).

Factor Investing:

Definition: Targeting specific factors known to drive returns, such as value, momentum, or size.

Strategy: Invest in funds or ETFs that focus on these factors to potentially achieve higher returns.

Thematic Investing:

Definition: Investing in funds that focus on specific themes or trends, such as renewable energy, technology, or healthcare innovation.

Strategy: Identify long-term trends and invest in funds that align with these themes.

Real Estate Investments

Real estate offers several advanced investment opportunities beyond simply buying and holding properties.

Real Estate Investment Trusts (REITs):

Definition: Companies that own, operate, or finance income-generating real estate.

Strategy: Invest in publicly traded REITs to gain exposure to real estate without the hassle of managing properties. Focus on REITs with strong fundamentals and high dividend yields.

Real Estate Crowdfunding:

Definition: Pooling funds with other investors to finance real estate projects.

Strategy: Participate in platforms that allow you to invest in commercial or residential properties with lower initial capital. Research the platform's track record and the quality of the projects.

House Flipping

Definition: Buying properties, renovating them, and selling them for a profit.

Strategy: Identify undervalued properties in desirable locations. Budget carefully for renovations and ensure the potential selling price justifies the investment.

Cryptocurrencies and Alternative Investments

Cryptocurrencies and alternative investments offer high-risk, high-reward opportunities.

Cryptocurrencies:

Definition: These are medium of exchange created and stored electronically on the block chain.

Strategy: Invest in a diversified portfolio of established cryptocurrencies like Bitcoin and Ethereum, as well as promising altcoins. Timely information about market trends and new technological is important.

Peer-to-Peer Lending

Definition: Lending money directly to individuals or businesses through online platforms.

Strategy: Diversify your loans across multiple borrowers to reduce risk. Research the platform's default rates and lending criteria.

Hedge Funds

Definition: Investment funds that employ various strategies to earn active returns for their investors.

Strategy: Consider investing in hedge funds if you have a high-risk tolerance and substantial capital. Hedge funds use strategies like long/short equity, arbitrage, and leverage to achieve high returns.

Conclusion

Advanced investment techniques can significantly enhance your portfolio's performance and diversify your investment strategy. By understanding and applying these strategies, you can optimize your risk-return balance and achieve your financial goals more efficiently. Remember, advanced investing requires continuous learning and staying informed about market trends and economic indicators. With careful planning and execution, these advanced techniques can be powerful tools in your wealth-building journey.

CHAPTER 6

Generating Passive Income Streams

These Passive income streams are a key factor to achieving financial Stability. Unlike active income, which requires continuous effort and time, passive income allows you to earn money with minimal ongoing work. In this chapter, we'll explore various passive income opportunities, including real estate, dividends, royalties, and building an online business.

The Concept of Passive Income

Definition: Passive income is money earned with little to no daily effort. It includes earnings from investments, rental properties, royalties, and other sources that generate income passively.

Benefits

Financial Independence: Passive income can cover your living expenses, reducing reliance on a traditional job.

Flexibility: With passive income, you have more control over your time and can pursue other interests or opportunities.

Wealth Building: Reinvesting passive income can accelerate wealth accumulation and help you achieve financial goals faster.

Real Estate for Passive Income

Real estate is a popular and effective way to generate passive income.

1. Rental Properties:

Definition: Purchasing properties to rent out to tenants.

Strategy: Invest in properties in desirable locations with strong rental demand. Ensure rental income covers mortgage payments, maintenance, and other expenses.

Benefits: Steady income stream, potential property appreciation, and tax advantages.

2. Real Estate Investment Trusts (REITs):

Definition: Companies that own, operate, or finance income-generating real estate.

Strategy: Invest in publicly traded REITs to gain exposure to real estate without managing properties. Focus on REITs with strong fundamentals and high dividend yields.

Benefits: Liquidity, diversification, and passive income through dividends.

3. Real Estate Crowdfunding:

Definition: Pooling funds with other investors to finance real estate projects.

Strategy: Participate in platforms that allow you to invest in commercial or residential properties with lower initial capital. Research the platform's track record and the quality of the projects.

Benefits: Lower entry cost, diversification, and potential for high returns.

Dividends and Stock Investments

Stocks that pay dividends can provide a reliable source of passive income.

1. Dividend Stocks:

Definition: Shares of companies that distribute a portion of their earnings to shareholders as dividends.

Strategy: Invest in established companies with a history of paying and increasing dividends. Reinvest dividends to buy more shares and compound your returns.

Benefits: Regular income, potential for capital appreciation, and tax advantages on qualified dividends.

2. Dividend Reinvestment Plans (DRIPs):

Definition: Programs that allow shareholders to reinvest their dividends to purchase additional shares.

Strategy: Enrol in DRIPs to automatically reinvest dividends and grow your investment over time.

Benefits: Compounding returns, no transaction fees, and dollar-cost averaging.

3. High-Dividend ETFs:

Definition: Exchange-traded funds that focus on high-dividend-paying stocks.

Strategy: Invest in high-dividend ETFs for diversification and steady income. Choose ETFs with low expense ratios and strong dividend yields.

Benefits: Diversification, passive income, and ease of trading.

Royalties and Intellectual Property

Earning royalties from intellectual property can be a lucrative source of passive income.

1. Book Royalties

Definition: Earnings from the sale of books, either through traditional publishing or self-publishing.

Strategy: Write and publish books on topics with a broad appeal. Market your books effectively to maximize sales.

Benefits: Long-term income, potential for multiple revenue streams, and creative satisfaction.

2. Music Royalties:

Definition: Earnings from the use of music compositions or recordings.

Strategy: Create and distribute music through various platforms

Benefits: Recurring income, exposure to new audiences, and creative fulfilment.

3. Licensing Intellectual Property:

Definition: Allowing others to use your intellectual property (e.g., patents, trademarks) in exchange for royalties.

Strategy: Develop valuable intellectual property and license it to companies that can commercialize it.

Benefits: Passive income, protection of intellectual property, and potential for high returns.

Building an Online Business for Passive Income

There various opportunities create passive income through online businesses.

1. Affiliate Marketing:

Definition: Earning commissions by promoting other companies' products or services.

Strategy: Build a website or blog with high-quality content. Promote products relevant to your audience and use affiliate links to earn commissions.

Benefits: Low startup costs, flexibility, and potential for high earnings.

2. E-commerce:

Definition: Selling products online through your own store or platforms like Amazon and eBay.

Strategy: Identify profitable niches and source products with high demand. Automate order fulfilment and use digital marketing to drive traffic.

Benefits: Scalability, flexibility, and potential for significant income.

3. Online Courses and Digital Products:

Definition: Creating and selling educational content or digital products (e.g., eBooks, software).

Strategy: Develop high-quality content that addresses a specific need or problem. Use platforms like Udemy, Teachable, or your own website to sell your products.

Benefits: Passive income, scalability, and potential for recurring revenue.

Conclusion

Generating passive income streams is a powerful strategy for achieving financial freedom. By exploring opportunities in real estate, dividends, royalties, and online businesses, you can create multiple sources of income that require minimal ongoing effort. Remember, building passive income takes time and effort upfront, but the long-term benefits are substantial. Stay disciplined, continue to educate yourself, and diversify your income streams to maximize your financial independence.

CHAPTER 7

Managing Debt Wisely

Managing debt is a crucial aspect of maintaining financial health and working towards financial freedom. While some debt can be beneficial, excessive, or poorly managed debt can lead to financial stress and hinder your wealth-building efforts. This chapter will explore the concepts of good debt versus bad debt, strategies for paying off debt, and the impact of credit scores on your finances.

Good Debt vs. Bad Debt

Not all debt is created equal. Understanding the difference between good debt and bad debt can help you make informed borrowing decisions.

Good Debt: This is debt that increase your net worth or generate future. It typically has a lower interest rate and contributes positively to your financial goals.

Benefit: Education can increase your earning potential and open career opportunities.

Student Loans:

Consideration: Choose loans with favourable terms and ensure the education will lead to a viable career path.

Mortgages:

Benefit: Real estate generally appreciates over time and owning a home builds equity.

Consideration: Ensure the mortgage is affordable and aligns with your long-term financial plans.

Business Loans:

Benefit: Financing a business can led to growth, increased revenue, and long-term financial success.

Consideration: Have a solid business plan and ensure the loan terms are favourable.

Bad Debt: Bad debt involves borrowing for items that don't generate income or appreciate. It typically carries high interest rates and can strain your finances.

Credit Card Debt

Drawback: High interest rates can lead to a cycle of debt that's hard to escape.

Consideration: Use credit cards responsibly and pay off balances in full each month.

Payday Loans:

Drawback: Extremely high interest rates and short repayment terms can trap borrowers in debt.

Consideration: Avoid payday loans and seek alternative financial solutions.

Auto Loans:

Drawback: Cars depreciate quickly, and auto loans often have high interest rates.

Consideration: opt for affordable, reliable vehicles and consider used cars to minimize debt.

Effectively managing and paying off debt requires a strategic approach. Here are some methods to help you reduce and eliminate debt:

Strategies for Paying Off Debt

1. Debt Snowball Method:

Definition: Focus on paying off the smallest debts first while making minimum payments on larger debts.

Strategy: List your debts from smallest to largest. Pay as much as possible towards the smallest debt while making minimum payments on the others. Once the smallest debt is paid off, move to the next smallest, and so on.

Benefit: Builds momentum and motivation as you see debts being paid off quickly.

2. Debt Avalanche Method:

Definition: Focus on paying off the debt with the highest interest rate first.

Strategy: List your debts by interest rate from highest to lowest. Pay as much as possible towards the highest interest debt while making minimum payments on the others.

Once the highest interest debt is paid off, move to the next highest, and so on.

Benefit: Saves money on interest payments over time.

3. Balance Transfer:

Definition: Transfer high-interest credit card debt to a card with a lower interest rate.

Strategy: Look for balance transfer offers with low or zero interest rates. Ensure the full amount is Pay off the before the expiry of promotional to avoid higher interest rates.

Benefit: Reduces interest payments and accelerates debt repayment.

4. Debt Consolidation:

Definition: Combine multiple debts into a single loan with a lower interest rate.

Strategy: Use a debt consolidation loan to pay off high-interest debts. Make consistent payments on the consolidation loan to pay off the debt faster.

Benefit: Simplifies debt management and reduces interest rates.

unlock the secrets to financial freedom and transform your future

5. Negotiating with Creditors:

Definition: Work with creditors to reduce interest rates, waive fees, or create a repayment plan.

Strategy: Contact your creditors to discuss your financial situation and negotiate better terms. Be honest and proactive in seeking a solution.

Benefit: Can provide immediate financial relief and more manageable repayment terms.

Credit Scores and Their Impact on Your Finances

The higher credit score is, the healthier in your finances. It affects your ability to obtain loans, credit cards, and even housing or employment opportunities. Understanding and improving your credit score can lead to better financial outcomes.

1. Understanding Credit Scores:

Components: Payment history, credit utilization, length of credit history, new credit, and credit mix.

Ranges: Typically ranges from 300 to 850. A higher score indicates better creditworthiness.

2. Importance of Credit Scores:

Loan Approval: Credit scores rating is one the key factor in assess the risk of lending money. Higher scores increase your chances of loan approval.

Interest Rates: Higher credit scores generally qualify for lower interest rates, saving you money on interest payments.

Insurance Premiums: Some of these insurance companies determine the premiums based on credit rating. Higher scores can result in lower premiums.

Employment Opportunities: A good credit score can improve your job prospects.

3. Improving Your Credit Score:

Pay Bills on Time: Consistently make on-time payments to build a positive payment history. Reduce Debt: Lower your credit card balances and avoid maxing out your credit limits.

Avoid Opening New Accounts: Limit new credit inquiries and accounts, which can lower your score temporarily.

Check Your Credit Report: This should be review regularly to ensure your credit report errors free and no dispute of any inaccuracies.

Conclusion

Managing debt wisely is essential for maintaining financial health and achieving financial freedom. By distinguishing between good debt and bad debt, employing effective debt repayment strategies, and understanding the impact of credit scores, you can take control of your financial future. Remember, managing debt is a continuous process that requires discipline and strategic planning. Stay committed to your debt repayment plan, monitor your credit score, and make informed borrowing decisions to pave the way for long-term financial success.

CHAPTER 8

Developing a Millionaire Mindset

Achieving financial freedom and building wealth requires more than just practical strategies; it requires a shift in mindset. Developing a millionaire mindset involves adopting the attitudes, habits, and behaviours that successful people use to create and sustain wealth. In this chapter, we'll explore the psychology of wealth, how to overcome financial fears and limiting beliefs, and how to cultivate the habits of successful individuals.

The Psychology of Wealth

The way you think about money significantly impacts your financial success. Understanding the psychology of wealth involves recognizing and adopting the mental frameworks that lead to financial prosperity.

1. Abundance vs. Scarcity Mindset:

Abundance Mindset: Believing there are ample opportunities and resources available. This mindset encourages risk-taking, generosity, and long-term planning.

Scarcity Mindset: Believing resources are limited and focusing on lack and fear. This mindset can lead to risk aversion, hoarding, and short-term thinking.

Adopting an Abundance Mindset: Focus on opportunities rather than obstacles, celebrate others' successes, and practice gratitude.

2. Growth vs. Fixed Mindset:

Growth Mindset: Believing skills and intelligence can be developed through effort and learning. This mindset fosters resilience and continuous improvement.

Fixed Mindset: Believing abilities are static and unchangeable. This mindset can lead to fear of failure and avoidance of challenges. Cultivating a Growth Mindset: Embrace challenges, learn from criticism, and persist despite setbacks.

3. Positive Self-Talk and Visualization:

Positive Self-Talk: Replace negative thoughts with positive affirmations about your financial goals and abilities. Visualization: Regularly visualize achieving your financial goals. This practice can boost motivation and clarify your vision.

Overcoming Financial Fears and Limiting Beliefs

Financial fears and limiting beliefs can hinder your progress toward wealth. Identifying and addressing these obstacles is essential for developing a millionaire mindset.

1. Identifying Financial Fears:

Common fears include fear of failure, fear of losing money, and fear of judgment.

Reflect on past experiences and messages about money that may have shaped these fears.

2. Challenging Limiting Beliefs:

Limiting beliefs are false narratives that restrict your financial potential (e.g., "I'll never be wealthy," "Money is the root of all evil").

Replace limiting beliefs with empowering ones (e.g., "I have the ability to create wealth," "Money is a tool for good").

3. Building Financial Confidence:

Educate yourself about personal finance and investing. Set small, achievable financial goals to build confidence and momentum.

Cultivating Habits of Successful People

Adopting the habits of successful individuals can significantly impact your journey toward wealth.

1. Setting Clear Goals:

Successful people set specific, measurable, achievable, relevant, and time-bound (SMART) goals. Break down long-term goals into actionable steps and regularly review your progress.

2. Practicing Discipline and Consistency:

Control your spending, adhere to saving, and investing to establish solid wealth.

Consistency in efforts, such as regular saving and continuous learning, leads to long-term success.

3. Lifelong Learning and Adaptability:

Successful individuals continuously seek knowledge and adapt to changing circumstances. Stay informed about financial trends, market conditions, and new opportunities.

4. Networking and Building Relationships:

Networking with like-minded individuals and mentors can provide valuable insights and opportunities. Building strong relationships fosters collaboration and support.

5. Giving Back and Practicing Gratitude:

Many wealthy individuals prioritize giving back to their communities and causes they care about. Practicing gratitude shifts focus from what you lack to what you have, fostering a positive outlook.

Conclusion

Developing a millionaire mindset is essential for achieving financial freedom and sustaining wealth.

By understanding the psychology of wealth, overcoming financial fears, and limiting beliefs, and cultivating the habits of successful individuals, you can create a solid foundation for long-term financial success. Remember, a millionaire mindset is not just about accumulating wealth but about creating a fulfilling and purposeful life. Embrace these principles, stay committed to your goals, and watch as your financial journey transforms.

CHAPTER 9

Crafting Your Long-Term Financial Plan

Creating a long-term financial plan is essential for achieving your financial goals and ensuring a secure future. A comprehensive plan includes setting and reviewing goals, planning for retirement, and considering how to leave a legacy. In this chapter, we'll explore how to craft a robust financial plan that guides you through various life stages.

Reviewing and Adjusting Your Financial Goals

Financial goals are the foundation of your financial plan. Regularly reviewing and adjusting these goals ensures they remain relevant and achievable as your circumstances change.

1. Setting Financial Goals:

Short-Term Goals: Achievable within a year (e.g., building an emergency fund, paying off credit card debt).

Medium-Term Goals: Achievable within 1-5 years (e.g., saving for a down payment on a house, buying a car).

Long-Term Goals: Achievable in 5+ years (e.g., retirement savings, funding a child's education).

2. Reviewing Goals:

Regularly review your goals to ensure they align with your current financial situation and life priorities. Adjust goals based on changes in income, expenses, or personal circumstances.

3. Tracking Progress:

Use financial tools or apps to monitor your progress toward each goal. Celebrate milestones to stay motivated.

Planning for Retirement

Retirement planning is a critical component of your long-term financial plan. It involves determining your retirement needs, exploring different savings options, and creating a strategy to ensure a comfortable retirement.

1. Estimating Retirement Needs

Calculate your desired annual retirement income, considering living expenses, healthcare costs, and leisure activities.

2. Exploring Retirement Savings Options

401(k) Plans: Employer-sponsored plans that offer tax advantages and potential employer matching contributions.

Individual Retirement Accounts (IRAs): Personal retirement accounts with tax benefits (traditional and Roth IRAs).

Pension Plans: Employer-provided plans that offer a fixed income in retirement (less common today).

3. Creating a Retirement Savings Strategy

The earlier you start saving the higher compound interest will yield. Contribute regularly to retirement accounts, aiming to max out contributions if possible. Spread your investments to lower risk and maximised return. Leaving a Legacy: Teaching Financial Literacy to the Next Generation

Leaving a legacy involves more than just passing on wealth; it includes imparting financial wisdom to future generations. Teaching financial literacy ensures your loved ones can manage their finances effectively and continue building wealth.

1. Educating Family Members:

Start financial education early, teaching children about saving, budgeting, and the value of money. Encourage teenagers and young adults to learn about credit, investing, and the importance of financial planning.

2. Setting Up Trusts and Inheritance Plans:

Consider establishing trusts to manage and distribute assets according to your wishes. Clearly outline inheritance plans in your will to avoid disputes and ensure fair distribution of assets.

3. **Encouraging Philanthropy**

Involve family members in charitable giving and community service. Establish a family foundation or donor-advised fund to create a lasting impact.

4. Documenting Your Financial Plan:

Keep detailed records of your financial plan, including goals, investments, insurance policies, and estate planning documents. Ensure that trusted family members or advisors have access to important information.

Conclusion

Crafting a long-term financial plan is essential for achieving financial stability and security. By regularly reviewing and adjusting your goals, planning for retirement, and considering how to leave a legacy, you can create a comprehensive plan that guides you through various life stages. Remember, a well-crafted financial plan is dynamic and adaptable, evolving with your changing needs and circumstances. Stay committed to your financial goals, seek professional advice when necessary, and take proactive steps to secure your financial future and that of your loved ones.

CHAPTER 10

Creating Multiple Streams of Income

Achieving financial freedom often requires more than one source of income. Diversifying your income streams provides financial security, reduces reliance on a single job, and accelerates wealth building. In this chapter, we'll explore various ways to create multiple streams of income, including side hustles, investments, and leveraging your skills.

The Importance of Multiple Income Streams

1. Financial Security Having multiple income streams protects you from financial instability if one source of income is lost. It provides a safety net during economic downturns or job loss.

2. Accelerated Wealth Building

Additional income can be reinvested to grow wealth faster. It allows you to pay off debt quicker and save more for future goals.

3. Diversification of Risk:

Different income streams can balance out fluctuations in the economy or specific industries. Diversifying income reduces the impact of adverse financial events.

Exploring Side Hustles and Part-Time Gigs

Side hustles and part-time gigs can be a great way to generate extra income without committing to a full-time job. Here are some popular options:

1. Freelancing:

This is a type of self-employment (creative writing, Online tutoring) on such platforms as Topal, Flex jobs, or Simply Hire

Benefits: Flexibility, control over projects, and the potential to earn a high hourly rate

2. Gig Economy Jobs:

Participate in gig economy platforms like Uber, Lyft, Door Dash, or Instacart.

Benefits: Flexible hours, easy entry, and immediate earnings.

3. Online Marketplaces:

Sell handmade goods, vintage items, or digital products on platforms like Etsy, eBay, or Amazon.

Benefits: Reach a global audience, minimal startup costs, and the ability to scale.

4. Blogging and Content Creation:

Start a blog, YouTube channel, or podcast on a topic you're passionate about.

Benefits: Passive income through ads, sponsorships, and affiliate marketing once you build an audience.

Investing for Passive Income

Investments can provide a steady stream of passive income, allowing your money to work for you.

1. Dividend Stocks:

Invest in companies that pay regular dividends to shareholders.

Benefits: Provides regular income and potential for capital appreciation.

2. Real Estate Investments:

Buy Properties that will generate income or purchase in real estate investment trusts (REITs).

Benefits: Rental income, property appreciation, and tax advantages.

3. Peer-to-Peer Lending:

Lend money to individuals or small businesses through platforms like Lending Club or Prosper.

Benefits: Earn interest on loans, diversify your investment portfolio, and help others achieve their financial goals.

4. Bonds and Fixed-Income Securities:

Invest in government or corporate bonds that pay periodic interest.

Benefits: Lower risk compared to stocks, regular income, and capital preservation.

Leveraging Your Skills and Knowledge

Monetizing your skills and knowledge can create additional income streams with minimal upfront investment.

1. Consulting and Coaching:

Offer consulting services in your area of expertise or provide coaching for personal or professional development.

Benefits: High earning potential, flexible hours, and the ability to help others succeed.

2. Online Courses and Webinars:

Provide Online training and courses or organise webinars on topics from your area of expertise.

Benefits: Passive income potential, scalability, and the ability to reach a global audience.

3. Writing and Publishing:

Write books, eBooks, or articles and publish them through platforms like Amazon Kindle Direct Publishing.

Benefits: Passive income through royalties, creative expression, and the potential to build a personal brand.

4. Public Speaking and Workshops:

Conduct workshops or public speaking engagements in your field of expertise.

Benefits: Earn money while sharing your knowledge, build your reputation, and network with industry professionals.

Conclusion

Creating multiple streams of income is a powerful strategy for achieving financial freedom and building wealth. By exploring side hustles, investing for passive income, and leveraging your skills and knowledge, you can diversify your income sources and increase your financial security. Remember, building multiple income streams takes time and effort, but the long-term benefits are substantial. Stay proactive, continuously seek opportunities, and invest in yourself to maximize your earning potential.

CHAPTER 11

Maintaining Financial Freedom

Achieving financial freedom is a significant milestone, but maintaining it requires ongoing effort, discipline, and adaptability. In this chapter, we'll explore strategies for preserving your financial independence, managing your wealth, and continuing to grow your assets over time.

Regular Financial Reviews

Regularly reviewing your financial situation is crucial for maintaining financial freedom and making informed decisions.

1. Annual Financial Check-Up:

Review your income, expenses, savings, and investments at least once a year.

Assess your financial goals and adjust them based on changes in your life circumstances or priorities.

2. Monthly Budget Review:

Track your spending and income monthly to ensure you're staying within your budget. Identify areas where you can cut costs or reallocate funds to savings or investments.

3. Portfolio Rebalancing:

Periodically review your investment portfolio to ensure it aligns with your risk tolerance and financial goals. Rebalance your portfolio by adjusting asset allocations to maintain your desired investment strategy.

Continuing Education and Adaptability

Staying informed and adaptable is essential for sustaining financial freedom in a constantly changing economic landscape.

1. Ongoing Financial Education:

Ensure that you update yourself on continuously basis about personal financing, investment, and economic situations. Read books, attend seminars, and follow financial news to stay updated.

2. Adapting to Economic Changes:

Be prepared to adjust your financial strategies in response to economic shifts, such as changes in interest rates, market conditions, or inflation. Be flexible and embrace new opportunities and threats.

3. Seeking Professional Advice:

Consider working with financial advisors, tax professionals, or estate planners to ensure your financial plan remains robust. Seek advice when making significant financial decisions, such as major investments or changes in your estate plan.

Managing Wealth and Lifestyle Inflation

Maintaining financial freedom involves managing your wealth responsibly and avoiding lifestyle inflation, which can erode your financial stability.

1. Avoiding Lifestyle Inflation

Resist the temptation to increase your spending as your income grows. Focus on saving and investing additional income rather than upgrading your lifestyle.

2. Smart Spending

Make thoughtful and intentional spending decisions that align with your values and long-term goals. Prioritize experiences and purchases that bring lasting value and joy.

3. Living Below Your Means:

Continue living below your means even after achieving financial freedom. Save and invest the difference to further grow your wealth and secure your financial future.

Giving Back and Philanthropy

Giving back to your community and supporting causes you care about can enhance your sense of fulfilment and purpose.

1. Charitable Giving:

Donate to charities and non-profit organizations that align with your values. Consider setting up a donor-advised fund to manage your charitable contributions.

2. Volunteering:

Volunteer your time and skills to support causes and organizations you're passionate about. Engaging in philanthropy can provide personal satisfaction and positively impact your community.

3. Establishing a Legacy

Plan how you want to leave a legacy, whether through charitable giving, establishing a foundation, or passing on your values and knowledge to future generations. Ensure your estate plan reflects your philanthropic goals and legacy wishes. Protecting Your Financial Freedom Safeguarding your financial freedom involves protecting your assets and preparing for unforeseen events

1. Insurance and Risk Management

Maintain appropriate insurance coverage to protect against health issues, disability, property damage, and liability.

2. Emergency Fund Maintenance

Keep your emergency fund replenished to cover unexpected expenses or income disruptions. Ensure your emergency fund is easily accessible and sufficient to cover at least three to six months of living expenses.

3. Estate Planning:

Ensure your will, trusts, and other estate planning documents are current and legally sound.

Conclusion

Maintaining financial freedom requires ongoing vigilance, discipline, and adaptability. By conducting regular financial reviews, continuing your education, managing wealth responsibly, giving back, and protecting your assets, you can preserve your financial independence and enjoy the benefits of your hard work. Stay committed to your goals, remain proactive, and continue to make informed decisions to sustain and grow your wealth over time.

www.ingramcontent.com/pod-product-compliance
Lightning Source LLC
Chambersburg PA
CBHW050233230526
45470CB00005B/1932